RECORD BREAKERS

ANIMAL KINGDOM

DAVID JEFFERIS

Belitha Press

First published in the UK in 2002 by

(B) Belitha Press

A member of **Chrysalis** Books plc
64 Brewery Road, London N7 9NT

Design and editorial production
Alpha Communications
Copyright © David Jefferis 2002

ISBN 1 84138 423 2

British Library Cataloguing in Publication
Data for this book is available from the
British Library.

10 9 8 7 6 5 4 3 2 1

Acknowledgements
We wish to thank the following
individuals and organizations for their
help and assistance and for supplying
material in their collections:
Alpha Archive, Liz and Tony Bomford,
Fred Bruemmer, Jane Burton, John
Cancalosi, Bruce Coleman Collection,
Corbis Images, Johnny Johnson, Janos
Jurka, Richard Kolar, Ben Osborne,
Sam Osolinski, Oxford Scientific Films,
Jeffrey L Rotman, Rick Price, Kim Taylor,
Terra Forma Globes, Jim Watt, Staffan
Widstrand, Norbert Wu

Diagrams by Gavin Page
Project modelling by
Emily Stapleton-Jefferis
Educational advisor Julie Stapleton

We have checked the records in this
book but new ones are often added.

Printed in Taiwan

▲ The grizzly brown
bear is the most
common bear in North
America. A full-grown
adult can weigh over
400 kg. The even bigger
Alaska brown bear can
weigh up to 800 kg.

Previous page: The lion
is Africa's biggest wild
cat. Adult males weigh
more than 200 kg.

CONTENTS

LOOK FOR THE ANIMAL SYMBOL

Look for the dog logo in boxes like this.
Here you will find extra facts and records.

WORLD OF ANIMALS

Our planet teems with animal life – on land, in the air and in the oceans. Scientists have studied nearly two million kinds of animal, but there are many others.

The smallest living creatures are tiny things called protists, most of which are far smaller than this full stop.

At the other end of the scale, the largest animal on our planet is the huge blue whale, which can grow to more than 30m long.

The biggest land animal is the African elephant. The heaviest one ever weighed over 12 tonnes.

▲ There are over 250 000 kinds of beetle, more than any other insect. Beetles live almost everywhere, except the oceans and icy polar areas.

▼ An adult male African elephant can grow nearly 4m high. He eats up to 350 kg of food every day.

▼ A giraffe's long neck helps make it the tallest land animal, at about 6m high.

▷ There are over 37 000 kinds of spider. The biggest is the goliath tarantula, which has a leg-span of up to 28 cm. The smallest spider is the patu marplesi of Western Samoa, which has a leg-span of just 0.43 mm!

🐕 MEGA WEB

Not all spiders make webs, but thousands of tiny money spiders made the biggest web ever seen. It was found covering the whole playing field of a school at Kineton in Britain.

tarantulas have very hairy legs

despite its length, a giraffe's neck has only seven bones, the same as a human's

▲ The kangaroo is the world's fastest hopping animal. Its huge back legs allow it to bound along at speeds of 65 km/h

▼ The cheetah from Africa is the fastest land animal. It can sprint after prey at up to 100 km/h.

ANIMAL MOVERS

Walking, leaping, hopping, swimming and flapping are just a few ways used by animals to get around.

The fastest animals are birds – some swifts can fly at more than 160 km/h in level flight. The fastest fish is the sailfish, which has been timed at more than 100 km/h. On land, the cheetah takes the speed record.

▲ The huge-finned sailfish has been timed at a speed of 109 km/h. The biggest measured weighed 64 kg.

▲ Some grasshoppers can leap 8m, about the same as a human jumping 200m!

The fastest land insect is reckoned to be the cockroach, which has been timed scuttling along at nearly 5 km/h. The dragonfly is the speediest flying insect. It can manage nearly 60 km/h.

cheetahs can run at top speed for only a short time

🐕 AMAZING MOVEMENTS

Water jet A cuttlefish squirts water back through a nozzle when it wants to move fast. The jet's force pushes it forwards.

Hanging on The gecko lizard has special foot pads that can grip on slippery surfaces. With these the gecko can climb walls and hang upside-down on a ceiling!

Loopy legs The looper caterpillar has two sets of legs, one at each end of its body. It arches its body in a loop, then digs in with its back legs, while the front ones stretch ahead. Then the back legs catch up again for the next step.

Fastest snake The black mamba can wriggle along at 20 km/h.

IN THE AIR

there are more than 100 000 kinds of butterfly and moth

▲ Hummingbirds are the smallest birds and the only ones that can fly backwards as well as being able to hover. This one is hovering by a flower to sip the nectar.

The first flying creatures were insects, millions of years ago. Today the skies are filled with all kinds of flying animals.

The smallest flying insect is a kind of mini-wasp called the fairy fly. It is just 0.02 mm long, small enough to squeeze through the eye of a needle. Compared to this, the biggest butterfly is a giant. An adult Queen Alexandra's birdwing of New Guinea has a wingspan of up to 28 cm.

The smallest bird is the bee hummingbird. It is named for the noise made by its fast-beating wings – 50 or more beats a *second*! The biggest bird of prey is the South American condor, which can weigh 12 kg. But flightless ostriches are much heavier, weighing up to 150 kg.

🐾 BIRD FACTS

Tiny bird The smallest hummingbird weighs less than 2g. Even the biggest is less than 27 cm long and weighs only about 20g.

Rarest bird The last wild Brazilian Spix's macaw disappeared in 2000. People are trying to breed them from a few specimens in zoos.

Big egg New Zealand's kiwi has the biggest egg compared with an adult bird. At more than 450g, a kiwi egg weighs nearly 25 per cent as much as its mother!

Quiet killer The owl is a good hunter at night. It has soft-edged wing feathers that give almost silent flight, just right for closing in on unwary prey.

owl's ears are hidden behind feathery tufts

a peregrine falcon folds its wings when diving on prey. The dive is called a stoop

birds of prey are called raptors. They have a sharp hooked beak

▲ The peregrine falcon can reach more than 300 km/h in a dive, making it the fastest animal of all.

▶ Swans have more feathers than any other bird. An adult has about 25 000 feathers, of which 20 000 very fine ones grow on the head and neck.

UNDERWATER LIFE

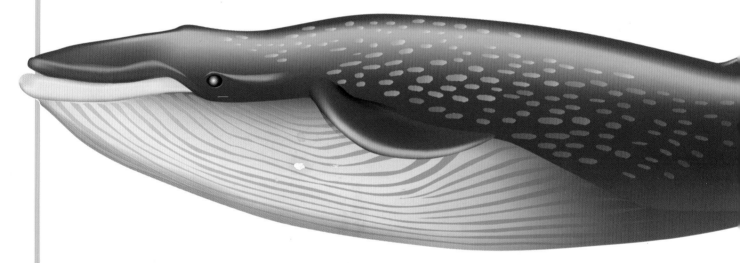

▲ Seahorses are thought to be the slowest fish. At full speed a seahorse covers only about 26 cm in a minute.

Water covers more than 70 per cent of our planet's surface. Living in the rivers, lakes, seas and oceans are more than 24 000 kinds of fish.

The smallest fish is the tiny dwarf goby, which measures about 8 mm long. The biggest fish is the 12m-long whale shark. It is not a vicious hunter though. Instead it is a gentle giant that cruises along with its mouth open, scooping up small creatures from the water.

The great white shark is reckoned to be the deadliest kind of shark. It has razor-sharp teeth and jaws that can rip off a 45-kg chunk of flesh in one bite.

The biggest animal in the sea is the blue whale. It is not a fish, but an air-breathing mammal. The huge creature feeds on tiny shrimp-like sea creatures called krill. An adult blue whale can weigh 150 tonnes or more, so its appetite for 4 tonnes of krill every day is not too surprising!

▲ The blue whale is the largest animal that has ever lived. Even giant dinosaurs were not as big!

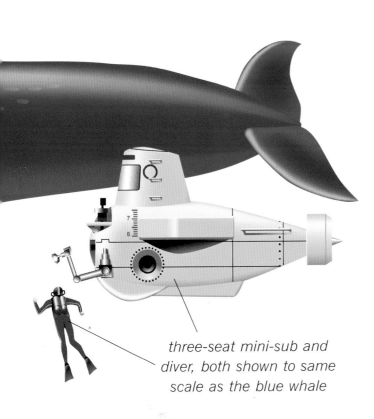

three-seat mini-sub and diver, both shown to same scale as the blue whale

▲ The whale shark is not normally a danger to humans. But one did swallow a Japanese photographer by mistake. The whale shark spat him out quickly and he escaped with scratches and bruises!

🐈 FISHY FACTS

Deep down The brotulid fish lives more than 8 km down. At this depth there is no light and the water pressure would crush you flat.

Big eyes The giant squid has the largest eyes in the animal kingdom. They can be more than 40 cm across in an adult.

Killer creature The stonefish of the Indian Ocean is the world's most poisonous fish.

ANIMAL SENSES

Senses are used to check on the world and for communication. Many animals have senses that are better than ours.

Bats have an amazing 'super-sense'. They send out high-pitched squeaks as they fly and can hear echoes that bounce back from solid objects, such as tree branches or the flying insects which they eat. Dolphins also use high-pitched clicking sounds to get an echo-picture of what's in the water nearby.

Many animals call loudly to attract mates. Tropical cicadas can be heard 400m away, while the loudest bird is thought to be a parrot from New Zealand. The male kakapo's deep call can be heard 7 km away!

▲ Bats are the best night-fliers of all. They use 'echolocation', a sense that allows them to find their way in the dark using sound instead of light. Here a bat hangs up to rest.

🐈 DANCE OF THE BEES

When a bee finds nectar, it can communicate this to other bees by making special dancing motions.

A bee dancing in a circle is showing that a source of nectar is not too far away. The bee can then wag its tail while running back and forth. This shows distance – the fewer runs there are, the farther away the nectar.

The bee can show which way to go by using the Sun as a compass, lining up its tail to point out direction.

◄ Bones in a dog's nose are covered in huge numbers of sensitive nerve endings. These give a sense of smell a million times better than that of a human.

▶ Night-flying moths are the insect world's champion sniffers. Males have feathery antennas that pick up the scent of a female up to 10 km away.

▼ A polar bear's sense of smell is so good that the bear can smell the rotting flesh of a dead seal 30 km away.

a polar bear's diet includes seal, walrus and fish

MEAL TIME

For many animals, life is short – it's kill or be killed by creatures bigger and faster than yourself. The top killers are carnivores – hunters that eat flesh.

▲ The world's fussiest eater is probably the koala from Australia. It lives on just one thing, eucalyptus tree leaves.

Some animals have to eat all the time. The smallest mammal – the tiny pygmy shrew – is one of these. It hunts for insects for 2–3 hours, has a rest, then looks for more food. If it doesn't eat for a day, it will starve.

But most animals can eat far less often than shrews. For example, a great white shark can survive for several weeks on one good-sized fish supper.

an adult locust is about 4–6 cm long

◄ The desert locust is a large grasshopper that lives in parts of Africa, the Middle East and India. When locusts swarm they become the most destructive insect in the world. Even a small swarm of 50 million locusts can destroy vast fields of crops, enough to feed 500 people.

▼ There are 41 kinds of wild dog, and the timber wolf is the biggest. These wolves hunt in a group or pack, working as a team to bring down big animals such as deer or caribou.

🐺 HUNTING IN PACKS

Fish herders Despite the name, killer whales belong to the dolphin family. They are ferocious hunters and work together in groups. One trick they use is herding fish to shallow waters. Then the killer whales take turns to gobble up the trapped fish without having to chase them.

Pack cat Lions are the only wild cat to hunt in a pack. Females do most of the hunting, but share their catch with males and cubs.

Hunting dog Along with wolves, dog hyenas are the best pack hunters. Hyenas make a kill on more than half their hunts.

a full-grown male weighs up to 80 kg

COLOURS AND COATS

Animals have colours that match their surroundings as a way of hiding. Some animals are camouflaged so well that they seem to almost disappear.

▲ Arctic hares live the farthest north of the rabbit family. In winter they have white fur to hide against the snow.

Camouflage is nature's way of letting an animal hide from others. For example, a tiger's stripes make it difficult to see in tall grass and a lion's brown coat matches the dusty African landscape. Other creatures hide almost perfectly – when a leaf insect stops moving it is almost impossible to tell it apart from a real leaf!

◀ Zebras have the boldest colours of any African plains animal. The stripes are a 'dazzle' pattern that makes it difficult for a hunter to see how many zebras there are in a group.

🐾 KINGS OF CAMOUFLAGE

Messiest spider The Australian bird dropping spider is so named because it looks like a smelly lump of bird mess.

Weediest fish The sargassum fish lives in the Sargasso Sea area of the Atlantic Ocean. It looks just like seaweed.

Creepy snake The vine snake is so thin that it looks like creeper or vine.

Some animals can change colour to match their surroundings. The best-known is probably the chameleon lizard. Its outer skin is naturally yellow, but can quickly change to patterns of green and brown. The secret lies in dark pigments that move in the skin, allowing the chameleon to match any leafy background.

▲ The chameleon can change its colour in a minute or two.

▼ The fastest colour-changer is the cuttlefish, which can speed through a rainbow of shades in less than a second!

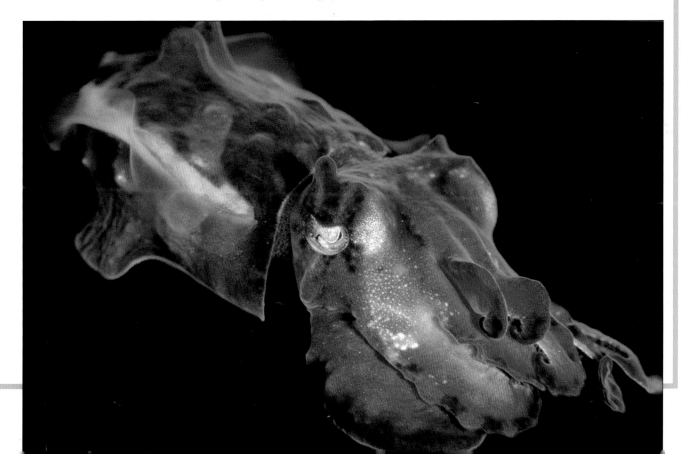

ANIMAL HOMES

Many animals build somewhere to live. It may be a simple hole in the ground or something much more impressive.

Birds are champion home builders, with nests ranging from a hummingbird's thimble-sized home to the bald eagle's 3-tonne giant.

One nest can even be eaten. The cave swiftlet builds a nest from spit. It dries to a whitish colour and can then be used to make a favourite Chinese dish – bird's nest soup!

Not all homes are built to last. Gorillas spend a few minutes each day making a sleeping platform, then move on next morning.

▲ The slimiest home belongs to the parrotfish. At night it covers itself with a nest of mucus from special skin glands. Next day the parrotfish eats up the slippery stuff and swims off.

🐾 NATURE'S BEST DAM BUILDER

The American beaver is famous for building dams across rivers and streams. The beaver has four huge front teeth that can chop down a small tree in minutes. It lays the wood in the water to make the dam. When the dam is finished, a pool of water builds up behind it.

Then the beaver can make its home, called a lodge, in the pool. The living quarters in the lodge are above water level, with underwater tunnels that lead to the outside world. In the lodge a beaver family has warmth and protection in winter.

beavers grow up to 80 cm long

▶ A beaver tows building material to its dam.

▲ Bald eagles make the biggest nests
in the bird kingdom. The largest
ever seen was 3m across and
more than 6m deep.

LONGEST JOURNEYS

▲ North American caribou make the farthest land-animal migrations. They walk about 1300 km every year to summer pastures in the Arctic regions of northern Canada. After eating the new-grown plants there, the caribou walk back south and spend winter deep in Canadian forests.

Many animals have no fixed home. They spend their lives moving, or migrating, long distances to reach fresh food supplies or for warmer weather.

Birds are the world's big long-distance travellers. Every year millions of them migrate around the world. Terns circle the world between the Arctic and Antarctic. Golden plovers fly 10 000 km between South America and Canada. Land animals such as the caribou also migrate, as do many sea creatures. The green turtle swims 2000 km to breed on an island in the Atlantic Ocean.

▶ Over its life, an arctic tern may fly more than 1 million km.

🐺 FLYING FROM POLE TO POLE

The arctic tern makes the longest migration of any animal. Terns breed in large colonies in the Arctic, when it is summer in the north. After breeding – they usually lay 1–3 eggs – terns fly off south, on a 20 000-km journey to Antarctica. By the time they get near Antarctica it is summer there. The terns spend the long days fishing off the coast, where they dive for fish and other small sea creatures. As summer ends, the terns reverse their journey and head north again, ready to start another breeding season in the Arctic summer.

Arctic

Antarctica

Route of the arctic tern

long wings are good for gliding flight

body grows up to 1.25m long

▲ The albatross has the longest wingspan of all birds. From tip to tip, its wings can measure 3.7m or more.

The wandering albatross covers great distances, though it stays mostly in southern seas. It eats squid and other sea creatures, drinks seawater and sleeps while floating on the surface. It visits land only for breeding.

▲ Monarch butterflies leave Canada in autumn to fly more than 3000 km to sunny Mexico.

LIFE SPANS

Most animals have shorter lives than humans, but a few outlive us. These include deep-sea tube worms and giant tortoises, both of which live over a century.

▲ Most insects live a short while, but the colourful jewel beetle can go on for about 30 years.

Few animals survive their full lifespan to die of old age. Most die young from accidents, disease or when killed and eaten by other animals.

Even if a wild animal manages to survive into old age, this has its own dangers. For example, old elephants often starve to death because their teeth fall out and so they cannot eat properly.

But there are a few animals that live for a long time. Some researchers claim that the giant turtle of the Pacific Ocean Galapagos Islands may live for over 200 years!

◀ Killer whales are the longest-lived mammals in the sea. Females can survive up to about 80 years, but males live only about 50 years. Killer whales are the fastest mammals in the sea. An adult can speed along at 55 km/h.

◀ With a lifespan of more than 60 years, elephants are the longest-lived land mammals, apart from humans.

🐾 FROM A DAY TO A CENTURY-PLUS

Only a day The mayfly lives for just a day or so when adult.

Long jumper Most kangaroos live about 5–7 years, but the oldest on record died at 23 years.

Longest-lived fish The lake sturgeon can reach 80 years old.

Oldest bird The wandering albatross can live over 70 years.

Ancient islander The lizard-like tuatara lives on islands off New Zealand. It can survive for 100 years or more.

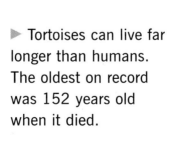

▲ Goldfish belong to the long-lived carp family. The oldest on record was a pet called Tish – it lived for 43 years.

▶ Tortoises can live far longer than humans. The oldest on record was 152 years old when it died.

EXTREME SURVIVAL

Surviving in very hot or cold places can be very tough. But many animals that do so have special features that allow them to lead normal lives.

▲ Siberia's tiny birch mouse survives icy winters by sleeping from early September to the following May. During its long sleep the mouse can lose about half its normal body weight of 12g.

There are lots of ways to survive the cold – many animals have thick fur, others dig holes for protection. Some forget winter altogether by finding a hole or cave, then going into a type of sleep, called hibernation.

When it hibernates, an animal's breathing and heart rate become very slow. It uses much less energy and may survive all winter using the fat stored from its last meals. All sorts of animals hibernate, including hedgehogs, squirrels, bats and toads. When they wake up in spring, they all go hunting, for they are *very* hungry!

◀ Foxes are the smallest members of the dog family. The arctic fox has thick fur, with short furry ears and fur on its footpads. With this natural overcoat for protection, it survives in temperatures far below freezing, often as low as -50°C.

🐕 DESERT SURVIVORS

Big drink Camels are able to survive using water from desert plants. They also drink huge amounts of water when they can, up to 50 litres at a time.

Below ground Some desert frogs and toads go underground, protecting themselves in a coat of spit or mucus. When it rains, they dig themselves out again.

Stinger The desert scorpion stings prey, then crushes it and injects a digestive fluid. The scorpion then sucks up the liquified prey – it needs no extra water supply to survive.

▲ The ice fish can survive in chilly water of -1.5°C. It has a natural antifreeze which stops its body liquids from freezing.

scorpion's sting is in its tail

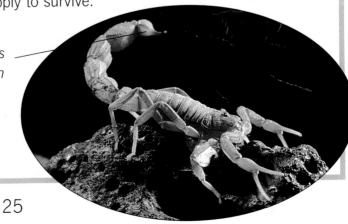

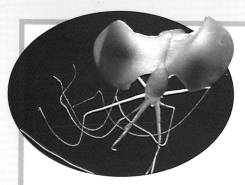

▲ The spidery squid.

ANIMAL RECORDS

Here are some facts and stories from the world of animals.

SPIDERY SQUID

In 2001 researchers found a new kind of squid, living as deep as 5 km below the surface. The mystery beast has longer tentacles than other squids. They are also far thinner than those of a normal squid and have an elbow-like bend. Researchers think the new squid trails its spidery tentacles in the water, waiting for small sea creatures to get caught in them.

MICRO LIZARD

In 2001 a new kind of lizard was found on the island of Beata, in the Caribbean Sea. The dwarf gekko is only about 16 mm long, making it the smallest lizard known.

The Caribbean is also home to other tiny creatures, such as the bee hummingbird and the world's thinnest snake, the threadsnake. It is so slim that if you could take the lead out of a pencil, the threadsnake could wriggle inside the hole!

SNAKES ALIVE

The reticulated python is a huge snake. The longest ever seen was more than 10m.

◀ The Siberian tiger is the biggest wild cat. Adult males may weigh more than 300 kg.

CREEPY-CRAWLY TERROR

The commonest thing for people to be frightened of is the spider, a fear called arachnophobia. Few of us like snakes much, but they are not as scary as spiders.

SLEEPY HEADS

Koalas are the champion sleepers of the animal kingdom. A koala typically spends about 22 hours a day sleeping. The slow-moving South American sloth comes a close second, spending 18–20 hours a day asleep.

FAST FLYER

The Australian dragonfly is the speed king of the insect world, having been timed hurtling along for a few moments at 58 km/h. Some flies and moths have been recorded flying at nearly 40 km/h.

MINI MAMMALS

The smallest horses are called falabellas. One of these stands just 47 cm high at the shoulder. The pygmy white-toothed shrew is the smallest mammal of all – the tiny creature is only 6 cm long.

SPRINTING OSTRICH

The world's biggest bird is the ostrich, which can stand nearly 3m tall. It cannot fly, but makes up for this by being the bird that runs fastest. An ostrich has been timed running across the plains of Africa at 72 km/h, with a stride of at least 7m long!

▲ Penguins are the deepest-diving birds and can stay under water for about 18 minutes. They live in Antarctica and fish in the icy waters there.

▼ The ostrich lays the biggest eggs. They can be 18 cm long and have as much yolk as 24 hens' eggs.

ANIMAL WORDS

▲ Terns flocking together before migrating south.

Here are some words used in this book that you may not know.

ANTIFREEZE

A liquid that has a lower freezing point than water. The ice fish has a natural antifreeze that allows it to live in icy waters without trouble.

ARCTIC

The area around the North Pole where it is cold and mostly ice-covered. The area around the South Pole is the Antarctic. Terns migrate between the poles every year.

CAMOUFLAGE

Colours and patterns used by various animals to help them blend into their surroundings.

CARNIVORE

An animal that eats the flesh of other animals. Many carnivores eat other things as well as meat. For example, bears enjoy gobbling up tasty berries in springtime.

▲ The eagle is a bird of prey, or raptor. This tame bird shows its sharp, hooked beak.

FLIGHTLESS BIRD

A member of the bird family that has wings too small for it to fly. Examples include the penguin, the ostrich and New Zealand's kiwi. Chickens are not quite flightless – a female has been timed in flight for a record-breaking 13 seconds.

HIBERNATION

A sleepy state in which some animals pass the winter – to avoid the cold and because there is little food to eat. An animal that hibernates lives on its body's fat stores during sleep. Some animals, such as bears, don't sleep all winter. They wake from time to time and eat food stored nearby.

MAMMAL

A warm-blooded animal that feeds its babies on mother's milk. Examples include bears, dogs, cats and humans.

MIGRATION

The route followed each year by an animal to find warmer weather and a better food supply. Migration routes can be very long – many birds fly thousands of kilometres, as do some mammals, such as the Canadian caribou, which walks to and from the Arctic.

PACK

A group of animals that hunts as a team. An example is the lion, which lives and hunts in a group called a pride. With teamwork the pride can chase and bring down a big animal such as a zebra.

▲ The grey whale migrates farther than any other mammal, on sea routes more than 20 000 km long.

PIGMENT

Colouring material in the skin. Pigments in a chameleon's skin allow it to change colour from yellow to green or brown.

PROTIST

A simple form of life, mostly no bigger than a dot, though some protists are larger. They come in all sorts of different shapes, from jelly-like blobs to things that look rather like micro-mushrooms.

RAPTOR

A bird of prey, such as an eagle. Raptors all have sharp, hooked beaks for tearing into their prey, as well as curved claws called talons.

▲ A tiny protist, seen through a powerful microscope.

ANIMAL PROJECTS

These experiments will help you find out more about the animals that live near your home.

There are billions of animals on our planet. Humans are outnumbered many times over, especially by creatures that are smaller than us. For example, there are likely to be many more spiders in your home than people. Take a closer look around – you could be surprised at what you find!

◀ Butterflies and spiders are common household visitors.

TAKE SOME SOIL SAMPLES

Many creatures live in the soil below your feet. They include tiny bugs, slithery earthworms and multi-legged centipedes. In this experiment you can take a sample of soil to see what's in it. If you like, wear a pair of rubber gloves to avoid getting your hands dirty.

1 You need a garden trowel, a clean sheet of paper and a magnifying glass. Wash and dry a glass jar to carry the soil sample and be ready to dig several times for specimens.

◀ Here a bee moves very slowly through grass in late summer.

▶ Frogs love damp places in quiet corners.

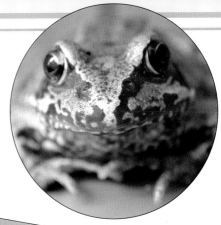

ANIMALS AROUND YOU

Making a regular wildlife report is a good way to get an accurate idea of what animals live around you.

The best plan is to look at the same time, once a week (or daily if you like) then collect the notes as a monthly report.

You will soon get a good idea of what the wildlife is doing where you live.

AUGUST - ANIMALS SEEN

Birds	Mammals	Other
Thrush x2		
Robin x1	Fox x1	Snail x8
Blackbird x2	Badger x1	Slug x4
		Spider x6

WILDLIFE NOTES Use a spiral-bound notebook, and mark your creature-count in columns. One page per month should be enough room.

2 Place soil in the jar. If you see a worm, put it in the jar, but take care not to harm it.

3 Empty the soil on to the paper sheet and inspect for interesting creatures.

4 Use the magnifying glass for a closer look. Put the soil back when you have finished.

INDEX